# The Chronicles of a Migrant

Ogechukwu Nwabulue

ISBN 979-8-89485-644-5 (Paperback)
ISBN 979-8-89485-645-2 (Digital)



Covenant Books
11661 Hwy 707
Murrells Inlet, SC 29576
www.covenantbooks.com

# Introduction

Life, they say, is not balanced. In every sphere of it, there is always good, bad, and ugly, with much to abhor and much more to cherish. Hoping to get a balance as I put them on a scale, I saw how impossible it was and then said to myself that life experiences and desired expectations can never be fully satisfying. What then? Sleep on it and just accept all it throws at me? No. I concluded that even if I do not have it all, at least I will keep adding to the good side of the scale, so that I might have more to my advantage. I came to this understanding when I migrated to the United States of America with my family. When I was still in Nigeria, I often had this fantasy image of how America was. But I came to its reality when I finally found myself in it.

I realized that people have different reasons for leaving their home country, but one reason can be generalized: greener pastures, a better life, which they hope to find. Every human being tends to desire a better life and can go the extra mile, making many sacrifices to get the better life desired. I remember when I was in school, I had a classmate. While we were discussing someone in the news who sold his inheritance to travel abroad, I asked him if he would do the same if he had the opportunity, and his response was, "Yes, I will. I mean, who wouldn't do it for greener pastures?" You can see how easy it was for him to decide because, to many—if not all—traveling abroad is seen as a chance of making life better. But then, as I got older, I discovered that not everyone who travels abroad experiences a better life. Some people face many difficulties that make their lives back home seem better, and because of shame, they cannot summon the courage to go back home. Some who eventually do return are faced with a more terrible situation of societal segregation and are left devastated.

I then asked myself, why do we, using my country as a case study, tend to see other countries as the best place to be? Why do we uphold situations there as better than ours? It is simply because Nigerian leaders, through their corrupt practices, have made every average Nigerian desire to leave the country. My country is naturally blessed with so many resources, both natural and human. If the leaders had managed and developed these resources well, I assure you no one will want to leave. My country is a beautiful place, and moreover, home is always the best, but many factors have made it seem like abroad is the best. I want to use this medium to advise anyone who is doing fine at home to consider intensively before wrapping up all their resources to travel abroad. Always give it thorough consideration. Look into the pros and cons—the good, the bad, and the ugly. Investigate properly where you are going. Conduct research on their culture, religion, laws, and so on, so you will not live a life of regret.

When we moved to the United States of America, I discovered that Europe and America are greatly overwhelmed by the influx of migrants, mostly from Africa. It hurts me that our people, including me, run away from our homeland to a place where the people don't seem to love us. I am unapologetic in making that comment because I am also a victim of racism and a firsthand witness to discrimination. Then I began to think: If the USA and Europe are feeling overwhelmed by the rate of migration to their lands, they should stop the marginalization of African countries and other third world countries, as they say, and allow them to develop what they have, so they can become independent financially and technologically. Though you might say they no longer rule Africa, they still interfere in our political matters, all for their political interest and pride, which keeps Africa where they want it to be—third world. It hurts me that they are taking all the best of Africa, the best of human and natural resources, leaving us dry. Nevertheless, the enemy outside cannot intrude until he aligns with the enemy inside. What do I mean by that? Simply put, the first people to blame are the African leaders, who, because of their selfish and greedy nature, allow themselves to be used, leaving their country at the mercy of the West.

This brings me back to my first question: Why migrate? Would I have migrated if things were working well in my country? Would I have migrated if life were flourishing in my country? Would I have migrated if our leaders were more like patriots rather than opportunists? The answer to those questions is obviously no, but here I am in another man's land, seeking purpose and a better life. Forgive me, Motherland. I will always have you at heart. I will never forget the moonlight tales, the dances and plays in the rain, the whistling of the birds on the paths to the stream, the fresh water flowing from rocks that gives a sense of satisfaction like fresh wine. Natural foods like oha soup, akpu, ugba, ona, and so on. The arts and crafts filled with rich cultural heritage. I pray earnestly and hope that the future generation will experience a national turnaround for good, so they will not be left with no choice but to leave.

I have met many people who migrated from different places, like Mexico and the Philippines. From my interactions with them, I discovered their reasons for migrating are also the same: a quest for a better life. I also discovered that every migrant, no matter how much better their life is here, still misses home. Home sweet home, they say, no matter how it is, is still home.

I have also come to the knowledge, through my findings, that the second reason people leave their country for another is because of war and civil unrest. I was interacting with a man I met at the grocery store, name withheld. He told me he was from Sudan and that he came to the United States because of the civil war that resulted in the division of the country into South Sudan and Sudan. He narrated his ordeals while traveling from country to country before finally reaching the United States, which was his end goal. He spoke of the near-death experiences he had. He said to me, "I took all those risks just to get here, and yeah, here I am, scared of visiting my country. But what can I do?" I saw the sadness, the sorrow, and the pain in his eyes. Though you might say he has found the better life he longed for, he is still not completely happy because he is disconnected, if not completely, from his origin and heritage.

*O leaders of Africa, why have you allowed your own to wander away? Why?* I leave that for you to ponder.

A lot of people run to the United States thinking it's a safe haven. Little do they know that there is no such place as a safe haven in this world. Every society has its security challenges. The difference only is the level of insecurity and the enforcement of laws in bringing accountability. For example, the United States has faced gun violence and mental health issues in recent times. Someone wakes up, picks up a gun, and begins to shoot people randomly. I was terrified the first time I heard on the news about the killing of innocent children in school by a teenage boy, along with many other cases of mass shootings in public places. So you see, no place is completely safe—rather, some places are more severe than others.

In every decision, there is hope for a good result, but that is not always the case because most decisions made in haste, without proper analysis and prayers, turn out opposite to our expectations. When moving to another country, it is important to keep in mind that you are meeting people different from you. Be ready to receive a cold welcome from them because you are an alien, and they will definitely assess you from a distance before coming close, if they come close at all. Migrants tend to assume they are going to a place better than where they are and thereby create an imaginary free flow of life. We should always remember that there is no country where money grows on trees, and there is no perfect society.

A judge in Texas, who was hearing the case of some migrants who were thrown out of a temporary shelter with no food or water, said to them, "I understand your grievances, but I am sorry to say that the state is overwhelmed with the budget of taking care of you. You don't cross over to America and expect to receive free food and housing. It doesn't happen anywhere." I agree with that statement.

# Chapter 1

After moving to the United States of America, I was embraced by cultural shock. It was one of the most difficult things I had to deal with when we migrated. The cultural differences were too many for me to understand, and it took me some time to adjust. Thank God I was not left broken because, trust me, some people were left emotionally broken because of the everyday struggles they could not handle. At first, I was disoriented and afraid. I would always say to myself, "Ogechukwu, will you be able to associate well?" Sometimes I found myself being aggressive, which was my way of reacting to my confused state, but that was not the right way. I knew if I continued this way, I would not only hurt myself but my family, too, who were looking up to me. So I quickly went to God in prayers because I knew he was the one in charge of my life.

The first culture shock I experienced was child discipline. In my country, we discipline children, and that helps to shape their moral upbringing. There are differences between child abuse and child discipline.

When you discipline a child, you are helping the child become morally principled, which makes for a healthy and strong society, and this we do out of love. We know that children need the guidance of an adult in everything they do, but in cases where a child is left to do whatever he or she wants, they will make a lot of devastating decisions that will destroy their lives and futures (Proverbs 22:15). But I will not overlook the fact that some adults and even parents abuse their children. That is something I do not support because every child who goes through abuse while growing up will have their future tampered with, and abuse is done out of hate. I also realized that anyone who has the heart to abuse a child—let alone their own child—must have been a victim of abuse and is sold out to the spirit behind such behavior.

But here in the States, they refer to discipline as abuse, which is not true. I believe it is because of their lack of discipline that has made a lot of children wild and have such moral degradation. Children now experiment with sex in the name of sex education, dress almost naked in the name of freedom, and change their biological nature in the name of "Be yourself, you are who you feel you are." *Hello!* If we can tell ourselves the truth, we will agree that society has become more dangerous since we took out moral instruction from our schools. In Nigeria, we believe so much in the phrase "Spare the rod, spoil the child" (Proverbs 13:24), and that has helped our children to a great extent.

Some days after we arrived, my sister-in-law called me over to the sitting room to chat. She began to orient me on how things are done here. The first thing she told me was, "Ogechukwu, we don't spank kids here."

I was like, "Excuse me."

She smiled and repeated, "We don't spank kids here in the United States. If you spank your child, they will arrest you."

I then asked her, "How then will you make your child know that what they did was wrong and keep them from doing it again if you do not spank them?"

She said, "You can talk to them."

Seriously? Talk to a child whose reasoning and understanding are not fully developed? "Hmmm! God have mercy on me," was my response because I could not imagine myself talking to my son, who may have skipped school without my knowledge. My first response as an African mother would be to get a whip as tall as he is and release a few strokes on his hand, then make him clean the whole house by himself for a month. When I am done with him, even if anyone entices him to do the same, he will say no.

Well, I am glad I stayed with her for some months, which helped me to adjust, and I will not forget the fact that God helped me too with applying wisdom in my disciplinary methods. May he be praised.

The second thing that got me was the American taxing system. I remember the first time I went to the store with my sister-in-law. I bought some clothes that cost approximately $45. At the checkout, I was told my total was $50. I told the cashier she must have made a mistake because I calculated the total amount of items I bought, and it was $45. She then asked me if I had added tax. I said, "Tax? What do you mean, please?" My sister-in-law tapped me from behind and whispered, "We pay tax for everything except food." Wow! I couldn't believe this. You mean I have to pay tax for every purchase I make? Okay, fine, even if you will tax, why not exempt the basic needs, which are food, clothing, and shelter? Why food alone? The cashier couldn't help but laugh. She must have noticed that I was a JJC. (In case you are asking what *JJC* is, it is fully written as "Johnny just come," a slang term we use in my country to refer to someone who is a novice.

It took me some time to get used to the taxing system. I remember the day I went to the store alone with just $15, believing I could get myself a good jacket. Thankfully, I did find one, and the price was $15. I was glad I had the exact amount, but I forgot that I had to pay tax. When I got to the cashier, she told me my money was not enough. I quickly remembered I hadn't included the tax, and unfortunately, that was the only money I had. I had no choice but to leave the jacket and walk away. I felt so embarrassed, but that was a great lesson for me because I never made that mistake again. It's called learning the hard way. Lol!

Now, it's not that the government of my country doesn't collect taxes. It's just that the way they do it is different. The producers who pay taxes include the consumer's tax in the prices. So, when you go to the store to purchase an item, the tax is included in the price, which means the amount you see on the tag is the amount you are paying. I think that is better—just my thoughts, though.

The third culture shock was learning to mind my own business. I know that might sound unusual to you, but yes, in my country, we are our brother's keeper. You know every neighbor by name, you know their children, their husband, the kind of business they do, and so on. Even if you decide to mind your business, your neighbor will not allow it because she will show up at your doorstep and say, "I just want to know how you are doing. Can I come in?" Tell me how you will not let her in. There is something we call "evening gatherings" where the men gather after a busy day to chat and enjoy some fresh air. That does not mean we intrude on people's business; no, we respect people's privacy. But it's a means of getting to know who is living next to you, and sometimes that helps create a sense of awareness of the environment. When you know who is in your community, you will be able to recognize when a stranger comes in to either steal or cause harm.

When we came to the United States, I was told to mind my own business because people here mind theirs. You won't believe that I have lived here for more than three years, but I don't know who my next-door neighbor is, much less whether they are tall or short. This sometimes makes you feel like you are alone in the world. Sometimes I ask myself, *Are there people in this house?* because you can hardly hear people talking. Thank God I have my family with me, because it would have been worse for me if I had come alone. My husband and kids make the days blissful, and Jesus makes me feel not alone. Glory to his name.

I was also marveled at the way most kids respond to their elders. In fact, forgive me for saying that here they don't have a culture of elder respect. Even the elders don't want the respect because they don't want to be reminded that they are old, forgetting that gray hair is a blessing. The Bible says in Proverbs 16:31 that gray hair is a crown of glory, which is earned in righteousness. Here, you will hear the kids say, "Hi, Dad. Hi, Mum." Oh my god! At first, I always got irritated by that when they said it to me, but I later got used to it. Trust me, it wasn't easy. I was taught to use the word *sir* when addressing an elder, but here you will hear things like "Ms. Carol" or "Mr. Mike," etc. When I tried to say it the way I was used to, they told me, "Oh come on, Oge! Loosen up. Stop using the word *sir*. You're not in the military. Be free." *Did you say "Be free"? I am free!*

*Can't you see I am only trying to show respect?* Hmm. Anyway, I am done because no one seems to understand.

A lady at my first job, whom I always addressed as "Ma'am," one day called me and said, "Oge, please stop using the word *ma'am* when you address me. Just call me Jane." I was baffled that she was getting upset because I was only trying to show respect. Well, I learned to understand that that is their culture. That is how they were raised, but don't blame me either. This is how I was raised.

Moreover, I was affected by the traffic rules, which made me afraid of going for a driving test. I took the bus for some months before I summoned the courage to go for driving lessons. In fact, my husband was the one who encouraged and pushed me because he kept saying to me, "I will not be driving you to places you want to go. You better go and learn how to drive because it will save me some stress." Indeed, he was right because some places I could have gone myself, he ended up going because I did not know how to drive.

The first day I started my driving lessons, I was taught so many road rules I had never heard of, and that made me worry if I would ever be familiar with them. Rules like bicycle lanes—back in my country, I had never seen or heard of a bicycle lane. I mean, everyone rides on the same road. Though I was able to get my license after many tries and failures, I am still not able to drive long distances, nor have I summoned the courage to take the freeway. Anyway, I am not bothered because I know I will get there someday.

Finally, I want to talk about the problem of food. Almost all the food we are familiar with is not sold at the regular stores here in the United States. Of course, we all know there are foods you can find everywhere, like rice, beans, potatoes, tomatoes, and so on, but there are native foods, foods that are peculiar to a particular people. These are the ones I am talking about. In my tribe (the Igbo-speaking Nigerians), we are known for fufu with native soups like oha, onugbu, okazi, and many others, and foods like ona, ukwa (breadfruit), ugba or ukpaka, and others. Though you can find them at some African stores, they are expensive, which is quite understandable, and that makes it difficult to maintain them as regular food.

What then can you do but learn to adjust your taste and desires to fit what you can find? There is a saying, "If the desirable is unavailable, then the available becomes desirable." I experienced the reality of that saying, though it wasn't easy for me because I am not a food adventurer. What I mean by that is I find it hard to try new foods. Some people I know can eat anything as long as it is edible, but I am so selective, even with our native foods sometimes. The day I asked my sister-in-law about stores that sell African foods, she said to me, "Oge, you have to learn to adjust your appetite. Learn to improvise. The sooner you start accepting the foods here, the better for you." So I started trying out some foods like tacos, mashed potatoes with gravy, and macaroni and cheese. Well, they are not bad. At least I was able to eat some, but they have never become my favorite. By God's grace, I usually manage to scrape together some money to get African foods, despite the high price.

What, then, am I saying? To Americans, they enjoy their tacos, macaroni, and so on, and I enjoy my fufu and oha soup, which shows how beautifully different we are made by God, proving his creative power, which cannot be replicated. No matter how unpleasant a food might be to you, don't forget that there are people who cherish it, which is something you have to respect and appreciate. *Selah*.

Finally, in this chapter, I won't leave out the language barrier many migrants face, especially those from countries with a primary language other than English. To some extent, I was not affected because I can speak and understand English. Nevertheless, I still faced difficulty understanding, especially when I came into contact with people who had accents. In my country, Nigeria, English is used as a central language. We have many languages and dialects, so English is used for general communication. This helps many people speak and understand English. Permit me to inform you that we have our own kind of English, which is called "pidgin English." It is a modified kind of English mixed with native language.

Back to my discussion. I met many people from Mexico and Asia who don't know how to speak or understand English. That is why many, when they arrive in the USA, enroll in English classes, which is a good decision because life can be a bit complicated and confusing if there is a language barrier. I remember the story in the Bible about the Tower of Babel. They were on the verge of accomplishing their quest to reach heaven, and God, seeing that, decided to confuse their language, and that was the end of the project. This shows you the power of effective communication.

Moreover, if you don't understand the language of the people you are living with, it will make you vulnerable to some avoidable dangers because you won't know when you are trespassing in places that clearly say "Do not trespass." Also, some bad people might try to take advantage of your ignorance to dupe or rob you. I thank God I 'm able to speak and understand English, because that helped me achieve certain things to some extent. I found myself in an advanced technological society, where my ability to read and write helped me navigate some rigorous paths.

# Chapter 2

Inasmuch as everyone who migrates to developed countries does so with the intention of getting a better life, that does not mean they are very poor in their home countries. Many people have degrees, and some have master's degrees and even doctoral degrees from their home countries. Also, I have seen a great influx of medical practitioners to the Western world because of the high pay and the need for medical professionals. What I am trying to say is that most migrants, especially from my country—because I am using Nigeria as a case study—are educated, but I have noticed that many don't have any medical background. Yet because of the financial benefits in the medical field, they all jump into it.

This raises the question of whether they have a passion for the job, to which most answers I get are "no." Well, I am not blaming anyone because I also discovered that the medical field is where you can easily get a job without much racial profiling. This means that no matter the level of education you have in your home country, it will be hard to get a job, even if you upgrade your degree by going back to school. So, instead of going to school to get a degree in your previous field of study, many transition to a medical course so they can stabilize financially, which I totally understand.

I must say also that it is not only African migrants who rush to the medical field. I realized that Filipinos also rush into it. In fact, they are dominating the field. A guy from the Philippines, who was my coworker at my first job, once told me that he wanted to be a journalist, but his mom told him he would be forever poor if he did not go for a course in medicine. He said he had always wanted to be a journalist, and he thought moving to America would give him the opportunity to fulfill his dreams. But he was discouraged by his mother, who felt he would not have good financial prospects if he ventured into it. Being the obedient child, he consented to his mum's pressure because he did not want to disappoint her, as she had made a huge sacrifice to bring him to America. Though he still has that hunger in him, he has lost hope of ever fulfilling that dream.

I, too, faced this challenge. It was the most difficult challenge I encountered as a migrant. I was completely confused and uncertain about what to do. Back in my country, I had my life and career going. I had already set a timeline for reaching my end goal, which was to become a professor in education. I had a degree in education and had started preparing for my master's before we eventually traveled. I knew what I wanted, how to go about it, and what route to take to get there. I had a job as a schoolteacher, which I loved. I was walking the path that would lead me to becoming the professor I desired. But when I arrived in the United States, I became disoriented. I had never been this confused in my life because I always had plans.

It took me four years of thinking and praying for God's direction before he became merciful to me and began to direct my steps. Glory to his name. At first, I was planning to continue with my education background, but when I reviewed the educational system here in the States, I saw that it was completely different from the one I was used to. In my country, we believe in child discipline, which helps correct ill behaviors, but in America, they don't.

As a schoolteacher in Nigeria, we always ensured that students placed under us were taught good behavior and how to practice it. If a child decided to act disrespectfully, there was always a way to discipline that child, which was not abusive in any way. Any form of abuse was taken seriously by the minister of Children's Affairs. For example, a child cannot comfortably distract the classroom while the teacher is present without receiving some form of punishment. This helped to raise respectful and well-mannered children. But here in America, it is quite different. Teachers cannot discipline a child because it will be termed abuse, which is punishable by law. So no one wants to correct a child anymore, and that is why the society is filled with a lot of misbehaving kids.

Sometimes, the parents are to blame. They forget that whatever a child becomes starts at home, which means that whatever they are—good or bad—you will be the first to reap it. I am not saying that we are perfect in my country. No, there is no such thing as perfection in this world, except when Jesus returns. But what I am saying is that to a great extent, we have well-behaved children who still hold on to the teachings and chastisements that helped shape them into the people they have become, because the Bible tells us in Proverbs 22:6, "Train up a child in the way he should go, and when he is old, he will not depart from it."

My husband's niece told me a story of a teacher who was physically abused by a student because the teacher had confiscated the student's phone, which was distracting the entire class during a lecture. This is just one of the numerous cases I heard about student misconduct in school, and how they get away with it without any punishment. How will that child know that what he or she did was wrong if you did not chastise them? Well, I will leave you to answer that for me. Seeing all this, I decided that it is a no for me to continue as a classroom teacher.

I was then told about the medical field—how it is the one field where I was guaranteed easy job placement and, of course, good pay. It was said to be the only way I could get a competing chance. *Oh! I get it.* Since I was not born here and did not have my educational background here, I am as good as uneducated. My educational qualifications and achievements from my country are not always recognized, so to make a living in the workforce, I had to start afresh. And even starting afresh is still not a guarantee because you will face racial profiling, especially if you don't have their English accent or name. That is why many, if not all, go into the medical field—because there, you can easily get a job.

In the medical field here in the United States, they have certification programs you can enroll in that don't take long to complete and can get you a meaningful job to start your life. That might sound very easy, but trust me, it wasn't that easy for people like me who dislike science subjects, except for biology (excluding the anatomy part) and agriculture. I dislike anything that has to do with medicine, blood, and injuries. It makes my heart ache. However, I do love taking care of people, which is natural for most Africans. We always take up the responsibility of caring for our sick family members. In Nigeria, for instance, there are no nursing homes like we have in America, which make it easier for someone who has a sick family member. My grandmother was cared for by my mother until she went to be with the Lord, and that is part of our culture.

Therefore, the caring part of the medical field, which is the least level, is not really a problem, but the attitude of those you are caring for is sometimes not encouraging. Some patients have the habit of cursing, hitting, and kicking, making the whole activity dangerous and sometimes overwhelming. Also, for someone like me who hates the smell of medications, I always feel nauseous because the whole atmosphere is filled with the smell of medication, which gives me negative energy all the time. Thank God who gave me the grace to work while seeking his direction on what path to take, because I knew deep down that no matter how much is in the medical field, it was not for me. But I was initially faced with that as the only option, as many I knew were in it, and the teaching aspect, which seemed like another option, had already been washed out of my heart.

I started at the lowest level because it was easy to get the certificate, and we needed to get a job quickly and secure our own house. Thanks to my sister-in-law, who harbored us for some months before we were able to stand on our feet. She was very supportive and never stopped being supportive. I owe her a lot, but I know I might not be able to repay her fully. God, who knows her good deeds, will surely reward her abundantly.

I remember my first day in class. As the lesson went on, the instructor, who happened to be Nigerian, paused and asked if I was okay.

I said, "Yes, why do you ask?"

She said, "You have been staring at one point without blinking, like someone lost in thought."

"Oh, really! But I am with you, ma'am," I replied.

She then asked, "What was the last thing I said?"

I stuttered and replied, "I'm sorry, ma'am, I can't remember."

"You see, you're completely out of this class," she responded. "Please, whatever it is that's bothering you, don't let it get to you. This is America, and you need to be active and strong in order to make it. Do you understand?"

"Yes, ma'am," I replied.

"Good. I'm advising you because I see you as my sister. Here, we work hard because we have families back home who are hoping and depending on us. Don't forget that."

I nodded in agreement and thanked her. She mentioned helping my family at home, which is one of the subtopics I will be discussing. Helping family members at home is one of the reasons I was even considering being a nurse in the first place. But then, despite the fact that the Lord instructs us to live a selfless and sacrificial life, I cannot be the Lord, who already died for everyone. *Selah!*

On my first day at work as a nurse assistant, I met a lady whom I respect and take as a mother. She was like a Godsend. She encouraged me because she noticed how uneasy I was. She said to me, "Don't worry, in a few days you'll get used to it. I too felt that way when I first started, but now I'm used to it. We are strong people," she continued, "There's nothing we can't do to keep life going." And yes, she was right. Africans are strong. God placed in us the ability to withstand any obstacles. I guess that was the reason I was able to work as a nurse assistant for so long.

As the months went by, I continued to think and refused to give up. I said to myself, *There must be another way, another way to make a living besides being a nurse.* People have different areas of strength and weakness. I know my strengths, and being a nurse is not one of them. There are other ways I can be useful to society and still maintain my sanity. I knew I needed to seek the Lord's help—the one who can make ways across the sea and make water flow in the desert, and the one who never fails showed up and gave me peace. May his name be praised.

# Chapter 3

The Bible says in Philippians 4:6, "Be anxious for nothing, but in everything, through prayer and thanksgiving, make your requests known unto God." Stress and anxiety are two major ways the devil oppresses ignorant and unsuspecting Christians. In the world we live in, there are many things that can cause stress, and one of them is finances. Everyone is trying to meet social essential demands like food, clothing, and shelter. Because of this, a lot of people, especially migrants here in the United States, work two jobs and hardly have time for themselves and their families.

I know of a colleague who has a family back home, and because she wanted to meet their demands, she worked two jobs to the detriment of her health. One day, while working, she slumped and was rushed to the emergency unit. Thank God she recovered because so many who fall that way end up in the grave. I bet that taught her a great lesson because she came to understand that life is once, and if anything happens to her, the living will go on living with little or no memory of her.

I will first discuss stress as an underestimated factor in overall good health. Stress, if not well managed, can cause physical and mental illnesses, which can lead to death. I came to learn about the power of stress when I first started working as a nurse assistant. I saw how unhappy a lot of people were with themselves despite having money to boast about. Through my discussions with them, I learned how they didn't feel good but had no choice but to keep working. I tried to talk to them, to encourage them to take life easy and not overdo the whole thing, but it seemed I was pouring water on a stone because people are stubborn and slow to learn unless they have first-hand experience.

I have always tried to learn from others and not wait until I experience something before I learn, which has helped keep me from many troubles. I said to myself that I would not join the rat race but would take one step at a time, in accordance with the strength the Lord has given me at any given point. I concluded that I would not go into anything that would cause me emotional or physical stress. Therefore, no matter the amount of money I could earn, I opted out of working double shifts. I mean, I have kids to take care of anyway. I have learned to live happily with what I am earning, no matter how little, applying the saying, "Cut your coat according to your size."

I discovered that many people are the ones attracting the ants to their backyard. What do I mean by that? Many don't know how to live a full life, even with the little they have. I always tell a friend of mine who finds it hard to save some money, "You and your husband make more money than my husband and I do"—she had told me how much she was making—"yet you don't even have $1,000 saved in your bank account." She told me she would start saving when she finished nursing school and started earning more. I told her, "If you can't save now, you won't be able to save later, no matter how much you make, because it's all evident in the way you spend. You can drive a $10,000 car and still be happy. Why go for the one that costs $40,000, knowing it will cost you almost everything you have to keep up with the monthly payments?" She couldn't answer because she knew what I was saying was true. All she could say was that I behave like a grandma from the '80s. Hmmm. Well, I'll accept that if it means I won't be in debt, which is one of the main reasons people become emotionally and physically destabilized.

I see a lot of our people doing jobs that drain them emotionally, physically, and even spiritually. Many no longer have time to pray because by the time they get home, they are tired, and they slump into bed and doze off. This is exactly what the devil wants—to make us live busy lives and forget that God is the one who gives life and abundance. One thing I know is that God says he will give his children rest, and financial rest is one of them. I began to seek God's face for his rest in every area of my life because I didn't want to be the busy bee or be struck by the arrow of busyness that has overtaken the country we find ourselves in.

Please don't misunderstand me. I am not in any way against hard work. Being stressed out is different from being hardworking. You can work hard and still have peace of mind, but when you become stressed, you lose your peace and tranquility, which is not good for your overall health. I know what I'm talking about, and people who go through this will also attest to it because deep down, they know this is not what they want for themselves. But because the job is bringing in money and they don't know what to do about it, it seems like they are forever caught up in it. But I want to tell everyone who will read this that it's still not too late to have the rest that Jesus assured his people. All you have to do is start making some adjustments. Map out time to meet with God, and he will guide your ways. His word says in Psalm 37:5, "Commit your ways in the hand of God and he will establish your plans."

Every job has bad days, especially when you are not the boss. But it is a totally different situation if you love your job. Let's say, for instance, that you love being a nurse. No matter the hiccups you experience some days at work, you will still go strong. But if you don't love the job, every day will be a bad day for you, even when there is no problem. That is what I'm against. It's the inner peace you have that energizes you through tough times and keeps you going without feeling overwhelmed. Don't rush into something because everyone is going there. Find your own path and walk in it, trusting God to establish it.

As I mentioned earlier, the reason many, mostly among immigrants, work two jobs and double shifts is to be able to pay bills. This leads me to the next point related to stress that I want to talk about: *anxiety.* Using my country as a case study, I discovered that the ability to pay bills is one of the many reasons people work so much, even when their bodies are telling them they need rest. Anxiety comes when one has many demands and wants that need finances, and it seems the money is not flowing as much as they want. This can lead to anxiety and make people take on extra jobs or hours to meet those demands, even though they could do without. They still let those things become necessities.

Among my Nigerian siblings, I discovered that competition is a big factor that brings about anxiety, making them work double shifts at the expense of their health. Everyone wants to belong. To be the first to own a house. To own the best house, the best car, and so on. Nigerian people are good at competition. You'll hear someone say, "Look how she talked to me—just a common CNA like her," and other stuff like that. It sometimes baffles me, but I've already made up my mind that I will never be moved by any of that. They can call me names like "local champion" or "village girl." I will not be moved by it. All my focus is on finding my right path with God— the ancient path destined for me, which brings the peace I seek, and when I find it, I know I will be forever settled

Unlike average Nigerian here, who wants to ride the finest car, live in the costliest house, buy the latest clothes, and flaunt the shiniest jewelry, I am content. To meet these desires, they put themselves under anxiety and work burnouts.

One more thing I said I would discuss is family members living back home. Every migrant, not just Nigerians, has family members who live in their home country, and sending money back home is one of the things they do to help family members who they believe are in worse situations than they are. Nigerians are culturally trained to look after family members like siblings and parents, including extended family like aunts, cousins, etc. We believe that no matter where you go, you should never forget the road that leads you home. We look after family members without being compelled. There is an adage that says, He who hears the cry of a brother should not run away." About 99 percent of people from my cultural background adhere to this saying. That's why you see many of them working very hard to meet their family's demands.

Nevertheless, despite the fact that we are trained to look after each other, it is still not a mandatory law that you must do it. But we see it as an act of being a blessing, in accordance with God's word, and we also believe that blessings come to those who do such. It is quite annoying, however, when you have a family member who wants to take advantage of this to drain you if you're not careful. They see everyone who is abroad as a money-making machine, forgetting that good money doesn't come easy. I use the word *good* because I know there are people who move abroad and become criminals and drug dealers because they think it will generate easy wealth, but they forget that every ill-gotten wealth disappears easily too and denies you peace. The Bible clearly says, "There is no peace for the wicked."

Let me quickly advise my country people who are at home to appreciate every little money they receive from anyone abroad. It costs a lot of people their sleep, playtime, and even rest to be able to save after paying their bills so they can send something home. They deny themselves luxury to send you money. What you owe them is your prayers and appreciation. Some work under very harsh weather conditions that would make you not want to leave the house, but when they remember they have families depending on them, they get up and go to work.

I came across a video on TikTok. A Nigerian lady on her way to work made a video crying bitterly and laying curses on Nigerian leaders. She was living in the cold part of the United States, where it snows heavily. She was standing under the snow, talking about how hard it was for her to go to work under such conditions. She said that if not for the bad leaders who made Nigerians poor, she wouldn't have found herself there. You can imagine the level of hurt that lady is experiencing for her to come online, but her family might be in Nigeria thinking she is enjoying life. No matter how much money she is making, she is still not happy because life in fullness is not only about money. The weather conditions she is living in are draining her inner peace.

I pray for anyone who is experiencing this same situation, or if there is anything that is draining your inner peace and, if not dealt with, might lead to depression. May you find Jesus, the giver of peace. Invite Him into your space, and you will be amazed how that which has been draining you physically, spiritually, and psychologically will be suppressed. If he did it for me, he can do it for you too.

Let me say it loud and clear. For everyone who is back home: It is not everyone who is enjoying life abroad. In fact, a lot of people are not. The only difference is that the government here has tried to make life easier for the people by providing good social amenities, but you must pay for them through the taxes that are deducted directly from your paycheck. That is why every well-meaning Nigerian will never cease to pray for our dear country because I believe if things are made right, a lot of people, including me, would prefer to go home rather than stay in a country where you are easily discriminated against. May God bless the good people of Nigeria, and may God bless our dear nation. *Shalom.*

# Chapter 4

A song by a Nigerian singer says, "The key to a good life is contentment and persistence." I believe he is trying to teach us to be content with what we have, because a life without contentment will be filled with anxiety and sadness. It will cause us to be under pressure all the time, as we will always want to measure up to society's demands, which are never-ending. That is why a lot of people live fake lives. They show off what they don't have, making others believe they are what they are not. If you are content with what you have, you will not be ashamed of people knowing it.

But then, even when we preach contentment, we do not discourage aiming for higher positions or levels. That is where persistence comes in. Learn not to give up easily because even God in his word encourages us not to give up but to keep working for a better life. In Proverbs 13:4, it says, "The sluggard craves and gets nothing, but the desires of the diligent are fully satisfied." What does it mean to be diligent? It means being constant in effort to achieve something. The word *constant* still draws us to our key word *persistence*—to not give up even when results seem slow in coming, and to stand firm on our end goal as the final destination.

I was able to draw my conclusion on fulfillment in life with these two words: contentment and persistence. I believe first you have to be content, for that is the source of your peace, which helps you generate the strength and sanity to take further steps toward reaching your end goal. If you are not careful enough to retain your sanity, you might end up taking steps that are not in alignment with what you actually want, causing you to realize in the end that you have just wasted many years doing nothing reasonable.

When I started working, I knew I was not where I wanted to be. I lacked inner peace, got easily irritated, and grumbled most of the time. I knew I needed to do something about it, or the devil would turn me into a sadist. So I went quickly to God in prayer, asking him to give me the grace to find peace even in the midst of turmoil, while I waited patiently for his direction on the next step to take. I wanted to be fulfilled in life, and if you had asked me then what I wanted, I would have told you I didn't know. The only thing I knew was that I was not there yet. I knew I can't trust myself but rather trust God, who already knew, before creation, what he had written about me. All I needed to do was find out what it was.

But while I waited for Him, I still needed peace and joy in doing the work I was currently doing, thanking God for making it possible for me to have something to do in the first place. You might ask me, "What gives a sense of fulfilment? How do you know you are fulfilled?" Well, my answer to that is that fulfillment walks hand in hand with joy. Anything I do with joy makes me healthy both physically and mentally. That is why you must inquire of God, because God is the only giver of joy. What gives me joy might not give you joy, and vice versa, because we are created differently and sent on different missions. So all you need to do is find out why you were made and walk that path.

It doesn't all come flashy, but believe me, if you are on the right track, even if it's not flashy like the world thinks, you will still have joy because it is God who gives joy. Paul says in Colossians 1:24, "Now I rejoice in my suffering." Doesn't that sound strange? How can someone rejoice in suffering? It's because he is walking on the path designated for him, and the joy he talks about is the kind that only God can give. I believe Paul had never been that joyful when he was busy persecuting Christians.

So, my dear friend, do not just quit your job for something else until you have inquired of God what he wants you to do, so that you will not end up right back where you started. I know of a man who studied to become a medical doctor, and after practicing for about ten years, he quit his job and went back to study journalism. He is now a travel journalist, and he said to me, "Now I have found fulfillment." Isn't that funny? There is no relationship between the two professions. I've come to know that a lot of people who graduated from school would change their profession after a few years of working if given the opportunity. We may have studied certain subjects due to the influence of friends or parents, and in the end, we discover we are walking the wrong path.

For migrants like me, who had a life going in their home country until they relocated, and it seems you are being forced into something you know deep down is not for you—do not give up on what you believe in because of other people's opinions. You can use that job as a stepping stone toward achieving your desired goal, but never settle for less. Some people said to me, "Ogechukwu, we have no choice here. We only live to survive." My answer to them is, "I refuse to live just for survival. I know if I stand for what I believe in and keep working toward it, I will get there, no matter how long it takes." The main thing is not giving up because you never know how close you are to your breakthrough.

My advice, then, to all migrants all over the world: Anywhere you find yourself, please do not settle for something that does not align with both your spiritual and career principles. Though they say, "In Rome, do as romans do," but I say, "In Rome, do as your people do." *Selah*.

I want to lay more emphasis on contentment because as I talk about persistence, I will not forget the power of contentment. Even as you know you have greater heights to achieve, you should allow the process to take its full course. The process, especially with God, takes time, so while you wait on him, you should learn to be appreciative of what you have, so that you will not make irreversible mistakes while trying to look for a better life. This is a problem many people have—lacking the ability to be patient. Everyone wants it now. Let me shock you: Waiting for God takes time. I don't know why, only God does, but I assure you it is worth waiting.

So while you are waiting, the number one thing that will keep you strong and joyful is being content with what you have. I've been there too, and it was very hard for me. I remember I never stopped praying, "God, please teach me to wait." I think that was what really helped me because if not for God's help in causing me to wait, I would have taken off, trying to prove to everyone that I am not a failure. Looking back, I thank God for his help, because I would have ended up on the wrong path with the wrong set of people.

Now do not get it twisted. I know you may be asking, "How do I keep pushing for the best when I am content with what I have?" That is actually a good question, and I hope to help you understand it better.

In my life's pursuit of destiny fulfillment, I discovered that I began to get anxious and overburdened. I wanted to get there as fast as possible, neglecting God's law of appointed time and season (Ecclesiastes 3:1–8). It caused me sleepless nights of thinking instead of praying. Even when I prayed, I found I was praying with anxiety, like I wanted God to do it now, which is very unrealistic because if you walk with God, you must learn patience and endurance.

The anxiety was hurting me emotionally, mentally, and spiritually because I couldn't find that place of rest, which was promised to us in Christ Jesus. So I changed my prayer to, "Please help me, God. Teach me to wait on You and take away the haste in my soul." What did God do? He came in and began to teach me contentment— learning to give thanks for what I have now. That gave me a healthy mindset to know and pursue the right way to achieve the things I was hoping for. I use the term *right way* because a lot of people in a hurry always fall into the devil's traps, which might look like the real thing, but in the end, you discover you have just sold your whole self to the service of the devil.

Contentment will help you during your waiting time and will enable you to wait for God's appointed time, which will always come. In his own word says in Isaiah 40:31 that those who wait on the Lord shall not be put to shame; rather, they will soar on wings like eagles.

Going back to my case study, which is Nigerian migrants in the United States, I have found that we tend to be tempted to compare our achievements with others, whether a friend, family member, or coworker. For instance, I know of someone who is a licensed vocational nurse. When she discovered that a close friend of hers had enrolled in a registered nurse program, she rushed to enroll in the same program. She told me, "I don't want her to start feeling superior." I said to her, "You are causing yourself harm by thinking that way because it might lead you to jealousy." She wouldn't have gone for the registered nurse program if her friend hadn't gone for it. The worst part was that she was not ready because of her tight schedule and limited finances, but her desire to catch up with her friend dominated her thinking so much that she didn't consider the odds.

What's my advice then? Quit the comparison and stop the competition because when we came into this world, we came alone, on a different path. So your life must be run alone, without any external interference or influence that draws negative energy. This will help us live every moment in fullness of joy and satisfaction.

# Conclusion

Having said all this, using my story and the stories of people around me to mirror what the life of a migrant looks like, I want to encourage everyone all over the world, not just my countrymen—those who have gone through a lot to see that their families experience a better life—to be of good cheer. Keep your gaze on heaven, where we will have rest from all the struggles of this world.

Do not allow fear to overtake you and keep you from exploring all that God has in store for you, as it tried to do with me when I was faced with so many fears of uncertainty in every area, including job searching. Sometimes I thought, *My African accent betrays me. I'll never get that job.* I believed that because of the way I speak, they wouldn't hire me. I remember during my externship program for the medical assistant course I took, I was on the phone with a patient who spoke to me rudely. She said in a very harsh manner, "Can you give the phone to someone who can speak good English? How can you come to the United States and not know how to speak good English? How disgusting," she thundered.

I was able to control myself and tried not to let her ruin my day. I gently apologized and transferred the call to someone who could speak with her. After that incident, I began to ask myself, *Am I that bad in English?* I know back home that English is one of the compulsory subjects in school, and that makes a lot of Nigerians proficient in English. I might not be as fluent as an American, but I am definitely not a novice. My boss, when she learned of the incident, told me not to feel bad about it—that the patient was just transferring her aggression onto me because she was angry about the amount she was charged for her treatment. I said, "Hmmmm!

Okay." Even if I had decided to feel bad, what difference would it have made? But I was able to regain and maintain my confidence. That I cannot speak your language as fluently as you do does not in any way make me less of a person or less brilliant. So I learned to hold my head high.

Will I conclude this book without speaking to the Nigerian leaders? Nay. Nigeria is a country endowed with many human and natural resources that, if well harnessed, will make our country the greatest in Africa. Talking about greatness, we boast of that because of our population and, perhaps, our landmass, but that is far from what greatness really is. To be great means to be economically and humanly developed and technologically advanced.

An American researcher in a recent analysis declared the Igbos, a tribe in Nigeria, as the most intelligent in all of Africa. Notwithstanding, I am not limiting my scope only to those of the Igbo tribe but to all the tribes in Nigeria, which together make up the whole country. I believe Nigeria is made great by God through the unification of all its people, each with different strengths, which, when brought together, give the nation the admiration of the world. Nigerian people are very intelligent and creative, and most of our creativity manifests during difficult situations. Instead of being broken by tough times, we are made by them. Creativity can turn what is supposed to make us sad into comedy, and in the end, we laugh. People say this is how and why we survive hard times, while others say it is the reason the leaders are ruthlessly embezzling resources— because the citizens are not taking anything seriously.

In any case, despite her intelligence and natural resources, Nigeria is still among the third world countries receiving aid instead of being the one giving aid. With the poverty rate increasing yearly, it is clear that things are not getting better. I keep asking myself why. Why has there been no change, but instead, worsening conditions? The answer is very clear: We have leaders who are corrupt, unpatriotic, selfish, and greedy.

They are unpatriotic because they do not have the country's best interests at heart. They do not care if the country sinks into poverty. They are selfish because they don't care about the masses who are languishing in poverty. I call them greedy because they are never satisfied with their looting of the nation's funds, enriching their fat bellies that never seem to fill, living in luxury through embezzlement at the expense of their fellow citizens, forgetting that they are there to serve, not to be served.

This is a sad situation that has made the name *Nigeria* itchy to every ear because of the wide range of corruption in the nation. Anywhere you go and identify as Nigerian, you will receive special screening, as you have already been tagged a criminal. Some, because of this, change their native names to sound more English to avoid being easily identified.

I therefore plead with the Nigerian leaders and all African leaders who misuse their countries' blessings to retreat from such acts because whatever a man sows, that he shall reap. Let's come together and make our nation great again by turning away from corruption, which has caused many people to leave in search of greener pastures, causing our nation to lose many intelligent citizens to other countries. When citizens leave with their intelligence, they end up growing the economy and manpower of that country, making our own country less productive.

How can we blame them for leaving when we did not create a favorable environment for them to exhibit their full potential? I make this clarion call to our leaders because I have discovered from my interactions with many that they are willing to return if the leaders make changes in the governing system. No matter how green a place is, home is the sweetest place to be.

I not only call on the leaders but also on all the citizens of our great nation to never forget that it takes everyone to build a nation. We must also work together with the leaders to make our nation the home we desire it to be. God bless Nigeria and all the people therein. *Shalom.*

## An Ode to My Nation

O Nigeria, my country
A land full of milk and honey
My heart pants always for you
As I remember your beauty anew
Across the seas far away
The tides have taken me astray
Still, I hear your voice in my sleep
Saying, "Why hast thou left me to weep?"
Lo, I pray day and night
Hoping for the dawn of your light
Weep not, most blessed land
For I see your salvation at hand
Where there is news of good tidings
And I shall return to the rejoicing

# About the Author

Ogechukwu Nwabulue is a native of Anambra State, Nigeria, and currently resides in California, USA. She holds a degree in social studies from the University of Nigeria, Nsukka, and a national certification in education from Nwafor Orizu College of Education, Nsugbe, Anambra State, in religion and social studies. She loves writing and has a great interest in storytelling. She is happily married with children.

9 798889 485644 5